The Appe␣␣␣␣␣␣␣
of Terrorism
and the
Belfast Agreement

Patrick J. Roche

Patrick J. Roche is Deputy Leader of the Northern Ireland Unionist Party (NIUP) and the NIUP Assembly Member for Lagan Valley. He holds degrees in economics and politics from Trinity College Dublin and from the University of Durham. He has published on Irish nationalism and the politics of Northern Ireland. These publications include three books on the 'Northern Ireland question' co-edited with Dr Brian Barton – *The Northern Ireland Question: Myth and Reality* (1991), *The Northern Ireland Question: Perspectives and Policies* (1994) and *The Northern Ireland Question: Nationalism, Unionism and Partition* (1999). In 1995 he co-authored *An Economics Lesson for Irish Nationalists and Republicans* with Dr J. Esmond Birnie. He is a part-time tutor in philosophy of religion and Christian ethics at the Irish Baptist College.

Foreword

This book is a clear and devastating analysis of the concessions to Irish nationalism and Sinn Fein/IRA terrorism in the Belfast Agreement.

The book deals with:

- The formation of the Adams/Hume pan-nationalist front.
- The political elevation and legitimisation of Sinn Fein/IRA terrorism in the Mitchell Report.
- The UUP capitulation in the Belfast Agreement to the fundamentals of Irish nationalism.
- The corruption of democracy and the rule of law in the Belfast Agreement.
- The Belfast Agreement and the destruction of the RUC.
- The legitimisation of Sinn Fein/IRA terrorism by business and church leaders.

Throughout the book the claims of Irish nationalism are rigorously demolished and the final section of the book outlines a basis for devolved government in Northern Ireland grounded on the intrinsic merits of unionism rather than on the appeasement of 'Irish republican' terrorism.

The armalite and the SDLP

The Union is in crisis. That raises a fundamental question. How did unionists get to be in the position that they are now in? The answer to that question goes back to the late 1980s. Between 1988-93 Hume and Adams forged the basis of a pan-nationalist coalition grounded on the shared SDLP and Sinn Fein/IRA objective of the political unification of the island of Ireland. But the pan-nationalist coalition created by Hume and Adams was also based on calculations

Armalite and ballot box

of mutual self-interest on the part of the SDLP and Sinn Fein/IRA. Under the leadership of Hume and Mallon the overriding commitment of the SDLP has been to Irish unity. The leadership of the SDLP has pursued a twofold policy over a period of three decades in the pursuit of this political objective. Firstly, the SDLP has directed a sustained propaganda against the RUC aimed at undermining the effectiveness of the RUC in the fight against terrorism. The objective of this SDLP propaganda war against the RUC is to establish the credibility of the SDLP claim that the IRA cannot be defeated and that the only way to end the IRA violence is to concede the political demand of Sinn Fein/IRA for Irish unity.

Secondly, the core feature of SDLP policy has been a combination of the public condemnation of terrorism with the political exploitation of IRA terrorism to achieve the objective of Irish unity that the SDLP shares with Sinn Fein/IRA. SDLP policy has in effect been based on the hard-core hypocrisy of a concealed 'armalite and ballot box' strategy. The exploitation of political violence by the SDLP to achieve the political objective of 'Irish unity' that the SDLP shares with Sinn Fein/ IRA has effectively been concealed by a subtle use of language. During the 1980s – and particularly from the New Ireland Forum of 1984 – the language of 'dialogue', 'consent', 'new Ireland' became the verbal stock-in-trade of so-called 'constitutional nationalists' and in particular of the SDLP. The Irish historian, Clare O'Halloran in *Partition and the Limits of Irish Nationalism* has explored the logic and political intent of this 'new rhetoric of Irish nationalism'. The political objective of this new, and on the surface apparently apolitical and conciliatory rhetoric, is to 'obscure and dissimulate' (to quote O'Halloran) the traditional irredentist claims of Irish nationalism.

These considerations mean that to uncover the real objectives of the SDLP and the major political parties in the Republic it is necessary to penetrate the contemporary language of Irish nationalism. How then does the 'new rhetoric of Irish nationalism' actually operate to 'obscure and dissimulate' the traditional political demands of old-time Irish nationalism? This can be explicated by reference mainly to the SDLP. The first move in this rhetorical game is to publicly attach the party to some fashionable political understanding such as 'post-nationalism' or 'progressive Europeanism'. This is precisely what the SDLP did particularly from the early 1980s.

The SDLP presented itself during the early 1980s as a 'post-nationalist' party. The core political connotation of this fashionable piece of political jargon was that the SDLP was able to present the public image of a party that seemed to have divested itself of commitment to the traditional goals of Irish nationalism. The public cultivation of a 'post-nationalist' image had also the advantage for the SDLP of helping to publicly align the party with 'progressive Europeanism'. This is the understanding that the process of European integration is divorced from 'old fashioned' and 'destructive' calculations of self-interest (which, of course, is nonsense) on the part of the member states of the European Union (EU). The process of European integration is understood from the perspective of 'progressive Europeanism' to have eroded the basis of inter-state conflict and consequently to have secured peace in western Europe. There is a 'post-nationalist' dimension to this type of thinking that envisages that the process of European integration will culminate (for its adherents) in the utopian outcome of the 'death' of the traditional nation-state.

The SDLP is not in any real political sense committed to this combination of 'post-nationalism' and 'progressive Europeanism'. The SDLP is absolutely committed to the old-time goal of Irish unity that the SDLP shares with Sinn Fein/IRA. For example, Sean Farren, now Minister of Higher and Further Education, Training and Employment and usually understood to be one of the more intelligent and pragmatic members of the SDLP, stated in the *Belfast Telegraph* of 27 April 1995 that 'the SDLP prided itself on its commitment to the historic...desire for home rule and separation from Britain'. This raises a fundamental question. How is it possible for the SDLP, without outward political contradiction, to combine the public and politically fashionable image of a party committed to 'post-nationalism' and 'progressive Europeanism' with a deep-rooted commitment to the 'historic desire' of traditional Irish nationalism for 'separation from Britain'?

The answer to this question lies in the content of what is often designated (with considerable justification) the 'single transferable speech' of the SDLP. This 'single transferable speech' has focused *ad nauseam* on the need for large-scale economic and political transformation on the island of Ireland. The objective of this all-Ireland economic and political transformation was to create the conditions on the island of Ireland that the SDLP considered necessary to end the 'conflict' between the two so-called 'traditions' of unionism and nationalism. The political implication of this SDLP understanding was that the conflict between the 'two traditions' was due to the 'failure' of Partition. This meant that for the SDLP there could be no 'internal solution' that underpinned the existing constitutional status of Northern Ireland within the Union.

The SDLP understanding of the need for all-Ireland economic and political transformation informed the deliberations of the New Ireland Forum of 1984. This was the basis of agreement between the SDLP and the political parties in the Republic on a 'new Ireland'. The 'constitutional nationalist' understanding of the 'new Ireland' agreed in the Forum retained the integrity of traditional Irish nationalism. The 'preferred option' in the Forum Report of 1985 for the 'new Ireland' was a unified Irish state. The so-called 'constitutional nationalist' position since the mid-1980s was that the proper way to bring about the 'new Ireland' was by a process of economic and political transformation that the SDLP 'single transferable speech' claimed had secured 'peace and reconciliation' in western Europe during the post-war decades.

This was the point at which the fashionable jargon of 'progressive Europeanism' and 'post-nationalism' was deployed by the SDLP to rhetorically package what was presented by the SDLP as the means of securing the universally approved goal of 'peace'. But the SDLP and other so-called 'constitutional nationalist' proposals for securing 'peace' were also understood by the SDLP and the political parties in the Republic to be the means for creating the conditions for the realisation of the old-time nationalist imperative of the political unification of the island of Ireland.

What were these proposals? The SDLP and the parties in the Republic developed proposals for extensive all-Ireland economic and social 'harmonisation' and 'integration'. This type of thinking informed the deliberations of the New Ireland Forum and by the late 1980s had developed into the nationalist understanding that the island should be developed as a 'single economy'. In the early 1990s the local Confederation of British Industry (CBI) expended considerable effort with the Dublin-based Confederation of Irish Industry (CII) in the attempt to provide substantive credibility for the 'single island economy' perspective. The local CBI contribution took the form of proposals for a Belfast-Dublin 'economic corridor' as the basis of economic development for the island as a whole. But the CBI/CII case for the 'economic corridor' (a piece of superficially plausible jargon) was based on gross exaggeration of the anticipated benefits in terms of employment and north/south trade flows.

The leadership of the local CBI was (and still is) probably operating to an agenda based on nothing more sophisticated than a combination of political naivety and gross economic miscalculation. This organisation represents an economic leadership that, despite (perhaps because of) a vast system of state subsidy, has not been able to raise the level of economic productivity in Northern Ireland to what is required to sustain a high level of economic performance and well-being in the province. But the nationalist exponents of the 'single island economy' were more clear-headed. The simple fact of the matter is that the 'single island economy' project was not driven by pragmatic economic calculation but by the ideological imperatives of Irish nationalism.

Professor Paul Teague in a contribution to *The Two Economies of Ireland* argued that proposals ostensibly for economic harmonisation in Ireland are best understood as 'surrogates for the building of new constitutional arrangements on the island'. That is indeed the case. The development of a 'single island economy' would, of course, require the development of all-Ireland political institutions (such as now exist

12

under the terms of the Belfast Agreement) to formulate and implement social and economic policy on an all-Ireland basis. The entire economic perspective of the 'single island economy' and John Hume's 'Europeanism' involved the ideological deployment of a rhetorically plausible economics to give credibility and persuasive political force to the imperatives of traditional Irish nationalism for the political unification of the island of Ireland. This rhetorical plausibility was reinforced by John Hume's claims (repeated *ad nauseam* despite their being nothing short of straightforward nonsense) that the all-Ireland political institutions demanded by the SDLP and the political parties in the Republic were similar to the institutions of the European Union.

Nevertheless, this was a particularly powerful rhetoric. Despite the traditional nationalist *realpolitik* directed towards Irish unity, the 'new Ireland' was packaged as a 'post-nationalist' solution to political conflict that would operate through institutions claimed to be similar to those that had brought about political and economic 'integration' and 'reconciliation' in western Europe. John Hume utilised this 'new Ireland' rhetoric with considerable effect for the cause of Irish nationalism in the European Parliament. Unionist opposition could be easily presented to the international community as opposition to 'peace' and even as 'anti-Europeanism'.

But for this entire rhetorical strategy to really work, Sinn Fein/IRA had to be brought on board. Obviously without Sinn Fein/IRA agreement this 'new Ireland' scenario could not be sold to a government of the United Kingdom as a means of securing an end to IRA terrorism. But at the same time without IRA violence or the threat of IRA violence there would be no problem to be solved. The so-called 'constitutional nationalists' have always been aware of Gerry Adams' dictum in *The Politics of Irish Freedom* that without 'the tactic of armed struggle' the 'issue of Ireland would not be an issue'. The SDLP are entirely aware that without IRA terrorism or the threat of IRA terrorism the issue of the unification of Ireland would be of no political significance to anyone other than to Irish nationalists.

The Downing Street Declaration and Irish 'pan-nationalism'

But by the late 1980s Adams was aware of the need to expand the political dimension of the Sinn Fein/IRA 'armalite and ballot box' strategy. By this time the republican leadership had come to recognise that substantive concession to the goal of Irish unity could only be negotiated between the United Kingdom and the Republic - not between a government of the United Kingdom and either the SDLP or Sinn Fein/IRA. The SDLP objective in the negotiations with Sinn Fein/IRA between 1988-93 was to get Sinn Fein/IRA to agree to the conditions required to establish a pan-nationalist coalition including the Republic. Hume's strategic thinking was that once the pan-nationalist coalition was in place then real negotiations could begin with the government of the United Kingdom.

The key to the formation of a pan-nationalist coalition involving both Sinn Fein/IRA and the Republic was an IRA cease-fire. The SDLP and the political parties in the Republic never really required an authentic renunciation of violence on the part of Sinn Fein/IRA and certainly not a handing in of IRA weapons and explosives that would have removed the threat of Sinn Fein/IRA terrorism. But what did the IRA demand as the conditions for a cease-fire? The IRA conditions for a cease-fire were set out in a Hume/Adams statement of 25 September 1993 and in an IRA statement of 3 October 1993. Hume and Sinn Fein/IRA required from the government of the United Kingdom recognition of what they referred to as the 'right of the Irish people to national self-determination' which excluded what Hume and Adams called an 'internal settlement'.

These requirements were fully met by the Major government. The Downing Street Declaration of 15 December 1993 which Major negotiated with Reynolds conceded a collective 'right of self-determination' or self-government to the 'people of the island of Ireland'. This simply means that the Downing Street Declaration conceded the very basis of Irish nationalism. Irish nationalism is based on the claim that there is a single nation or 'people' on the island of Ireland with a 'right of self-determination' or self-government. This concession in the Downing Street Declaration to the very basis of Irish nationalism undermined the legitimacy of the status of Northern Ireland within the Union and reduced unionism to a so-called 'tradition' within the Irish nation. The logic of these concessions on the part of a Conservative government to the absurd nationalist claim that there is one nation on the island of Ireland was reinforced in the Declaration by Major's 'reaffirmation on behalf of the British government that….they have no selfish strategic or economic interest in Northern Ireland'. The Downing Street Declaration represented not merely the betrayal of the Union but also a massive appeasement of IRA terrorism.

Conceding the Union

The IRA announced a so-called 'cease-fire' on 31 August 1994 and on 22 February 1995 Major and Bruton agreed the Framework Document. The Framework Document was in effect a guarantee to Sinn Fein/IRA and to the SDLP of the structure of the all-Ireland institutions that would result from any negotiations. The guarantee of a virtually pre-determined outcome to negotiations was further underpinned for nationalists by the high-profile involvement by 1995 in the so-called 'peace process' of the Clinton administration. The policy of the Clinton administration was (and is) directed by an Irish-American caucus highly sympathetic to Sinn Fein/IRA. Senator George Mitchell represented this Irish-American caucus in Northern Ireland. That is why the Mitchell Report of 22 January 1996 backed a further Sinn Fein/IRA demand that Sinn Fein should be admitted to negotiations without any requirement for the IRA to surrender its terrorist arsenal. Both the

SDLP and the Republic also backed this Sinn Fein/ IRA demand. The objective of the so-called 'constitutional nationalists' in backing the Sinn Fein/ IRA demand to retain their terrorist arsenal was to maintain a credible threat of IRA terrorism in order to provide nationalist direction and dynamic to the negotiations.

The Mitchell Report and the legitimisation of IRA terrorism

The Mitchell Report is in fact a terrorist charter. The Report is based on the nationalist claim that a 'political settlement' is required 'to take the gun out of Irish politics'. This was the core position of the Sinn Fein/ IRA submission on 19 December 1995 to the Mitchell Commission. It is important to grasp the logic of the Mitchell Report. The claim that a political settlement is required to 'take the gun out of Irish politics' has two fundamental implications. Firstly, the terrorists must be included in the negotiations since the objective of the negotiations is to reach a 'settlement' acceptable to the terrorist. The Mitchell Report put Sinn Fein/IRA centre stage. Secondly, the Mitchell Report established the principle that there can be no requirement to decommission the terrorist arsenals until (if even then) a political settlement has been reached that is acceptable to Sinn Fein/IRA. That is why paragraph 34 of the Mitchell Report merely **suggested** that 'the parties should **consider** an approach under which some decommissioning would take place during the process of all-party negotiations'.

Paragraph 34 of the Mitchell Report does not contain any requirement to decommission and does not differentiate Sinn Fein from any of the other political parties in terms of a specific responsibility with respect to the issue of decommissioning. This means that the Mitchell Report gave substance to the republican claim that Sinn Fein is distinct from the IRA and should be given democratic parity with all other parties. The Mitchell Report followed through the logic of the recognition of the republican claim that Sinn Fein is distinct from the IRA. The Report established the fiction that Sinn Fein could be authentically committed to the so-called 'Mitchell principles' of 'democracy and non-violence' while the IRA refused to decommission its terrorist arsenal.

These considerations mean that the Mitchell Report was an exercise in the political elevation and legitimisation of terrorism. The Report went as far as to claim in paragraph 25 that 'there is a clear commitment on the part of those in possession of...arms to work constructively to achieve full and verifiable decommissioning'. The claim by the Mitchell Commission that there was within the IRA a 'clear commitment' to achieve 'full and verifiable decommissioning' was entirely without foundation. There are two possible explanations for this claim in paragraph 25 of the Mitchell Report. The first is that the claim was intended to achieve the political objective of facilitating the participation of Sinn Fein in the negotiations on the 'settlement' that the Mitchell Report claimed was essential to 'take the gun out of Irish politics'.

The second possible explanation is that the Mitchell Commission completely misread the strategic

Corruption of democracy

intentions of the IRA. The Mitchell Report was published on 22 January 1996. But by that time the IRA had already put in place the logistics for the resumption of a campaign of bombing on the UK mainland. The IRA exploded a massive bomb at Canary Warf on 9 February 1996 (a fortnight after the issue of the Mitchell Report) which killed two people and caused £85 million worth of damage to property. The major contribution of the Mitchell Report to the politics of Northern Ireland was to lay the foundation for the corruption of democratic practice and of the rule of law which was required to accommodate the Sinn Fein/IRA ideology of terror within the so-called 'peace process'.

George Mitchell was appointed chairman of the negotiations at Stormont Castle on 6 June 1996. Tony Blair became Prime Minister on 1 May 1997 and on 16 June 1997 the IRA murdered Constable Roland

John Graham and Reserve Constable David Johnston in Lurgan. On 20 June 1997 the IRA announced a second so-called 'cease-fire' and within a matter of weeks Sinn Fein was admitted to the negotiations on 15 September 1997. The UUP remained in the negotiations. This was a major capitulation on the part of the UUP on the issue of decommissioning and on the political and moral propriety of negotiating with the representatives of armed terrorists.

The Belfast Agreement and the mythology of Irish nationalism

The Belfast Agreement was signed on 10 April 1998. The Agreement is imbued with the ethos of Irish nationalism. The sub-text of the Belfast Agreement is that there is a single sovereign nation on the island of Ireland with a collective 'right of self-determination' or self-government. This was taken directly from the Downing Street Declaration. The sovereignty attributed in the Belfast Agreement to the 'people of the island of Ireland' is incompatible with a claim to sovereignty over any part of the island of Ireland by the parliament of the United Kingdom. That is why Annex A of the Agreement repeals the 1920 Government of Ireland Act and why the Northern Ireland Act of 19 November 1998 supercedes 'all previous enactments' including the 1800 Act of Union.

Further, in the Belfast Agreement the 'Irish nation' is defined in terms of the 'people of the island of Ireland'. This definition of the 'Irish nation' in the Agreement establishes the island of Ireland as the territory of the 'nation' or 'people' of Ireland. This means that the amendment of Articles 2,3 of the Republic's constitution set out in Annex B of the Agreement cannot be understood to remove the core territorial claim of de Valera's 1937 constitution. This is precisely the understanding of the amendments to the Republic's constitution in the Agreement set out by Ahern in a speech to the Dail on 21 April 1998. Ahern categorically assured the Dail that 'we are reformulating Articles 2,3 not abolishing them...the nation is not territorially disembodied...it is defined in clear terms as a thirty two county entity'. But this is a straightforward contradiction of the repeated claim by the UUP leadership that negotiated the Agreement that the 'Irish government had been forced to drop its territorial claim' (*Ulster Unionist Voice*, June 1998).

The Agreement incorporates the core political mythology of Irish nationalism that there is a single nation or 'people' on the island of Ireland with a right of self-government. The understanding that there is a single nation on the island of Ireland is constitutive of Irish nationalism and is therefore shared by Irish nationalists from Garret FitzGerald to Gerry Adams. For example, Garret FitzGerald has claimed in *Towards a New Ireland* that 'history has created on the island of Ireland one nation' and Gerry Adams in, *The Politics of Irish Freedom,* claimed that 'Ireland is historically, culturally and geographically one single unit'. The claim that Ireland is geographically a 'single unit' would indeed be difficult to dispute but that is of no political significance. The rest is straightforward nonsense – but nonsense that has motivated and sustained the hatred that has driven nationalist terrorism and murder on a staggering scale.

The absurdity of these nationalist claims is easy to demonstrate. There are two approaches to the determination of national identity that may be abstracted from the literature on nationalism. The objective approach focuses on criteria such as ethnicity, language and religion. The subjective approach stresses the consciousness of belonging to a single nation deriving from a distinct common culture and a shared understanding of the past or collective historical memory. Typically both approaches are combined in nationalist ideology and this is the case with Irish nationalism.

The simple fact of the matter is that these criteria cannot be used to establish the Irish nationalist claim that there is a single nation on the island of Ireland. The traditional nationalist use of religion to differentiate the 'Irish nation' in terms of Catholicism was self-defeating for the simple reason that a significant section of the inhabitants of the island are Protestant. But despite the secularisation of Irish society over the past three decades this religious identification grounded the sectarian hatred that has directed and sustained IRA terrorism and atrocity. This is one of the most significant themes in the disclosure of the mentality of Irish 'republicanism' in Sean O'Callaghan's book, *The Informer* and in Eamon Collins' book, *Killing Rage*. For example, O'Callaghan records a conversation with the IRA leader, Martin Ferris, on the La Mon atrocity. This conversation impressed on O'Callaghan the 'deep hatred' of Protestants imbibed from a 'bastardised and hate-filled version of Irish history' that Ferris displayed:

> During the conversation I asked Ferris about the reaction to 'bad' IRA operations, citing the La Mon restaurant atrocity in particular. The La Mon restaurant in County Down had been the target of an IRA firebomb attack in 1978...Twelve people were burned to death

in the resulting inferno. Ferris said to me, 'I don't know what all the squealing was about. They were only Orangies anyway'.

The nationalist claim that the inhabitants of the island constitute a common ethnic or racial group is even more nonsensical than the identification of the Irish nation in terms of Catholicism. This is an understanding that the historian A.T.Q Stewart appropriately dismissed in *The Narrow Ground* as something that 'ought to have been laughed out of court at the outset'. The appeal to language is particularly difficult for Irish nationalists since the logic of this criterion would virtually reduce authentic membership of the 'Irish nation' to the dwindling inhabitants of the Gaeltacht. But this appeal to language has been reinforced by the claim that the 'Irish nation' may be differentiated, to include all the inhabitants of the island, in terms of a distinct and ancient culture which in various ways is understood to have been fractured by Partition.

This theme of 'cultural unity' is a stock argument employed by nationalist politicians – particularly Charles Haughey in his political heyday – against Partition. For example, Haughey's St. Patrick's Day 'message' on 17 March 1981 is a standard example (bordering on the hilarious) of the theme of a distinctive 'cultural unity' extending throughout the entire island of Ireland:

> Except perhaps for the eagerness with which the Irish accepted St. Patrick's divine message, nothing is more remarkable about his missionary journey to this welcoming land of ours than the homogeneity of a cultural and social life he found wherever he went ... Because Ireland at the time of St. Patrick and for many centuries afterwards possessed a

cultural unity transcending its petty political divisions, the partitioning of their land was and remains an almost inconceivable eventuality to the vast majority of Irish men and women.

The notion of a 'cultural unity' extending over many centuries is a nationalist myth. This is reinforced by the fact that despite historical interaction within a small island over many centuries the inhabitants of Ireland do not share a common understanding and evaluation of the past that is the cement of national solidarity.

Nationalists have been reduced to using a form of geographical determinism in an attempt to produce a national identity that would embrace all the inhabitants of the island. The idea is that geographical location of birth determines national identity. This absurd notion indicates the extent of the intellectual bankruptcy of Irish nationalism. Nevertheless it was transplanted with the full approval of the UUP/UDP/PUP negotiators from the Downing Street Declaration into the Belfast Agreement. The Agreement states that 'it is the entitlement and birthright of every person born on the island of Ireland, which includes its islands and seas, to be part of the Irish nation'. The ponderous precision and legal tone of this language conveys the impression of substantial statement when in fact the content is simply nonsense. The intellectually impoverished appeal to geographical location of birth as the determinant of national identity simply obscures what Professor John A. Murphy stated with brutal clarity in the *Sunday Independent* of 31 October 1993. Professor Murphy argued that reference to a single Irish nation was 'tired old 1918 nationalist prattle ... there is no such political entity as the Irish people'.

The entire Irish nationalist attempt to undermine the legitimacy of the constitutional status of Northern

Ireland within the Union represents a retreat from reality into a fictional past. This exemplifies the self-deception that Clare O'Halloran in *Partition and the Limits of Irish Nationalism* sets out as a core characteristic of Irish nationalism. But this characteristic self-deception is not without considerable import for an understanding of Irish nationalism. The divorce of Irish nationalist ideology from political and economic reality has given rise to the passion and fanaticism that marks the so-called 'republican movement'. This passion and fanaticism can in turn only be sustained by retreat into the self-enclosed morality of the nation. But in this self-enclosed morality of nationalist ideology right and wrong are determined by what nationalists understand to be instrumental to the goal of the political unification of Ireland. The logic of this retreat into a self-enclosed nationalist morality is that there is no recognition of moral restraint on the use of force in terms of the norms of civilised behaviour or the moral imperatives of the Judaeo-Christian tradition. But in the absence of such constraint there is no moral barrier to terrorism and therefore to the catalogue of Irish nationalist atrocity extending over the past three decades.

These considerations mean that in the Belfast Agreement the UUP/PUP/UDP leadership conceded the very substance of an intellectually and morally bankrupt Irish nationalism. Where does that leave unionism? The clear sub-text of the Belfast Agreement is that unionism has fractured the sovereign will of the so-called 'people of the island of Ireland'. The imperative that is central to the Agreement is that the integrity of this 'national will' must be restored. This imperative is incorporated into the amended Article 3 of the Republic's constitution. The amended Article reads that it is 'the firm will of the Irish nation...to unite all the people who share the territory of the island of

Mechanism for Irish unity

Ireland'. Ahern stated in a Dail speech of 21 April 1998 that 'the new Articles provide a realistic mechanism for bringing about Irish unity'. But the UUP negotiators claimed that the Agreement, which includes the amended Articles, had 'secured Northern Ireland's place within the United Kingdom' (*Ulster Unionist Voice*, June 1998). This claim demonstrates that the UUP leadership that finally accepted the Agreement was either entirely devoid of political integrity or so politically stupid that they did not understand the content of the Agreement that they recommended to the unionist electorate in the Referendum and the Assembly elections.

The Belfast Agreement and the mechanisms of Irish unity

The paramount thrust of the Belfast Agreement is towards 'Irish unity'. That raises the question of unionist consent. The Agreement states that ' it would be wrong to make any change in the status of Northern Ireland save with the consent of a majority of its people'. This is the 'consent principle' in the Belfast Agreement. But this 'consent principle' is not based on any recognition of the validity of unionism in the Belfast Agreement. Indeed, the statement of the 'consent principle' makes absolutely no reference to unionists or to unionism but to a 'majority of the people of Northern Ireland'. The so-called 'consent principle' in the Belfast Agreement is a somewhat limited recognition on the part of nationalists that 'Irish unity' would be self-destructively unstable (and therefore, in the words of the Agreement, 'wrong') without at least the agreement of a majority of the citizens of Northern Ireland.

The Belfast Agreement contains the politically pragmatic recognition on the part of nationalists that without at least majority consent in Northern Ireland 'Irish unity' would simply not work. But this recognition is entirely compatible with the deliberate pursuit of the objective of bringing about the economic and political conditions and the all-Ireland administrative structures that nationalists consider would create the conditions in which majority consent in Northern Ireland would be forthcoming. This is the fundamental political 'game-plan' of the Belfast Agreement. The SDLP and Sinn Fein/IRA have a shared understanding of the Belfast Agreement that is also the understanding of the political parties in the Republic. Sinn Fein/IRA and their so-called 'constitutional nationalist' fellow-travellers understand the Agreement as providing the transitional institutions which they consider are required to bring about the conditions for majority consent in Northern Ireland to 'Irish unity'.

The North/South Ministerial Council is the core institution of the Belfast Agreement because the nationalist objective is that the structures of an expanding all-Ireland administration will develop through the operation of the Council. The Sinn Fein/IRA and indeed the SDLP (what is now the difference?) understanding of the role and the political significance of the North/South Ministerial Council was set out in the *Republican News* of 16 December 1999 which stated that:

> The first meeting of the All-Ireland Ministerial Council here in Armagh, truly marks the beginning of a new political reality on the island of Ireland. Republicans are now part of a new political administration, with elected representatives from throughout the island. The importance of thinking, planning and acting on an all-Ireland basis cannot be overestimated. We look forward to

strengthening and developing this work in a dynamic and energetic fashion.

The North/South Ministerial Council is the meeting place for Executive Ministers and Dail Ministers to formulate policy on an all-Ireland basis. The terms of the Belfast Agreement required that prior to the formation of the Executive at least twelve areas of 'north/south co-operation and implementation' had to be agreed. The Assembly approved on 16 February 1999 the twelve areas agreed for 'north/south co-operation and implementation'. New all-Ireland Implementation Bodies for six of these areas of 'north/south co-operation' were also approved by the Assembly on 16 February 1999. The remaining initial six areas of 'north/south co-operation and implementation' will be administered through relevant existing bodies in Northern Ireland and in the Republic.

The North/South Ministerial Council and the six Implementation Bodies were operationally established on 2 December 1999 when the Executive was formed. The North/South Ministerial Council and the Implementation Bodies are secured in international law on the basis of formal agreement between the government of the United Kingdom and the government of the Republic as required by the Belfast Agreement. These requirements of the Belfast Agreement relating to the areas of 'north/south co-operation and implementation' guaranteed that on the day that the Executive was formed (2 December 1999) the Executive would have an all-Ireland dimension of responsibility.

The North/South Ministerial Council and the all-Ireland Implementation Bodies lock the government of the Republic into every area of devolved government in

Northern Ireland. This is reinforced by the fact that the Intergovernmental Conference involves the Republic in non-devolved areas of policy affecting Northern Ireland such as policing, security policy, prisons, criminal justice and international relations. The UUP election literature for the Assembly elections claimed that 'the Stormont Agreement has scrapped the Anglo-Irish Agreement and will close Maryfield' (*Ulster Unionist Voice*, June 1998). But the UUP conveniently omitted to inform the unionist electorate that the Intergovernmental Conference and its Secretariat effectively incorporated the entire substance of the Anglo-Irish Agreement into the Belfast Agreement.

The simple fact of the matter is that the North/South Ministerial Council and the Intergovernmental Conference provide the Republic with an extensive and expanding input into the formulation and implementation of policy for virtually every aspect of life in Northern Ireland. The implementation of the Belfast Agreement has in effect established a de facto joint authority. The involvement of the Republic in the North/South Ministerial Council and in the Intergovernmental Conference will be directed by the 'constitutional imperative' ('It is the firm will of the Irish nation...to unite all the people who share the territory of the island of Ireland') explicitly incorporated into the new Article 3 of the Republic's constitution that Ahern described in a Dail speech of 21 April 1998 as the 'will of the Irish nation to unity'.

But the North/South Ministerial Council also locks the twelve Executive Ministers (including the First and Deputy First Ministers) into all-Ireland structures for policy formulation and implementation required within the terms of the Belfast Agreement. The development of policy for the twelve areas of all-Ireland 'co-operation and implementation' is an essential component of the responsibilities of the Executive. These considerations are reinforced by the fact that no department could be effectively operated in isolation from the other departments. The Executive is intended to produce an integrated structure of government. This means that each Minister must be substantively involved with the other Ministers in the running of his/her department and in contributing to the formulation of the annual programme of government and the budget allocations that must be approved by the Assembly as required by the Belfast Agreement.

The commitment of each Minister of the Executive to 'discharge effectively and in good faith all the responsibilities attaching to his/her office' and in particular to 'support, and to act in accordance with, all the decisions of the Executive Committee' is required by the Pledge of Office that each Minister must affirm as the condition of taking office. This pledge of office in effect ties each Minister into a commitment to implement the working of the core institutions established under the Agreement. These considerations clearly mean that no Minister could use the Executive as a centre of opposition to the implementation of the core all-Ireland aspects of the Belfast Agreement. The same applies to the statutory committees that have the somewhat menial function of 'assisting and advising' the Minister.

Participation in the structures of government – specifically in the Executive and in its statutory committees – established under the Belfast Agreement involves not mere acquiescence (which from an authentic unionist position would be bad enough) in the implementation of the Agreement but active participation in the implementation and outworking of an Agreement intended to lay the basis of Irish unity. This is very significant from the point of view of the nationalist understanding of unionist consent. The unionist participation in the negotiation and implementation of the Belfast Agreement is almost certainly regarded by the SDLP and by Sinn Fein/IRA as a confirmation of their shared understanding of how to secure unionist consent. The nationalist position – articulated on virtually every page of John Hume's 1996 book, *Personal Views: Politics, Peace and Reconciliation in Ireland* – is that unionists have no right of veto over the implementation of the means that nationalists consider are required to produce the unionist consent to 'Irish unity'. This is also the understanding of 'unionist consent' in the Labour Party policy document, *Towards a United Ireland* that was co-authored by Mo Mowlam.

Advocate of Irish Unity

The understanding that unionists have no right of veto over the means that nationalists consider are required to obtain unionist consent to the political unification of the island of Ireland is obviously based on an extreme nationalism that completely rejects that there is any validity to be attached to unionism. This is precisely the mentality that drives the terrorism of Sinn Fein/ IRA. But this is also the mind-set of the so-called 'constitutional nationalists'. For example, the *Forum Report* presented unionist objections to unification as an irrational amalgam of 'fears' and 'concerns' based on alleged unionist misperception of what the Report understood to be 'reality'. Clare O'Halloran, in her outstanding analysis of Irish nationalism in *Partition and the Limits of Irish Nationalism* clearly articulated the function for nationalists of this type of stereotypical treatment of unionism in the Report:

> Like already established unionist stereotypes, the image of the fearful northern Protestant (the dominant stereotype of unionists in the Report) had, as its primary function, the belittling of opposition to unity and in the context of the reiterated suggestion that unionist perception was inaccurate, the alleged anxieties were portrayed as irrational and groundless.

The nationalist understanding of unionism as the outcome of irrational 'fear' and misperceptions of 'reality' has been reinforced in contemporary anti-unionist polemic by a morally pejorative presentation of unionism. For example, Joseph Lee in his monumental, *Ireland: Politics and Society, 1912-85*, grounds the unionist resistance to unification in a 'Herrenvolk mentality'- unionism, for Lee, is the political expression of nothing more commendable than a 'racial imperative'. John Hume developed this type of anti-unionist polemic in a more personalised and characteristically unsophisticated way in his *Personal Views: Politics, Peace and Reconciliation in Ireland,* in which Hume presented unionism as the politics of a 'petty people'.

But there is a clear corollary to this understanding that unionism is the political outcome of the irrational 'fears' and morally reprehensible prejudices of a 'petty people'. The corollary is that, if necessary, unionists should be coerced into accepting the implementation of the means that nationalists consider are necessary to produce unionist consent to 'Irish unity'. Sinn Fein/IRA and the so-called 'constitutional nationalists' have fully embraced this commitment to the coercion of unionists. That is the whole point of thirty years of Sinn Fein/IRA terrorism directed against the unionist community in Northern Ireland.

The disposition to the coercion of unionists also lurks within the mind-set of so-called 'constitutional nationalism'. For example, John Hume was reported in the *Observer* of 27 April 1986 as demanding that the Thatcher government must 'lance the Protestant boil' in the face of unionist opposition to the implementation of the Anglo-Irish Agreement. That was not an isolated comment. Barry White records in his book, *John Hume: Statesman of the Troubles* that Hume disagreed with Faulkner on the need to talk to the leaders of the Ulster Workers' strike in 1974. Hume's response to Faulkners's suggestion was, according to White, that 'I'll sit here until there is shit flowing up Royal Avenue...and then we'll see who wins'. This obscenity fully displays the *realpolitik* of the Irish nationalist mind which is, quite simply, to bury unionism.

But the Belfast Agreement has removed the need to coerce unionists. The so-called 'constitutional nationalists' who produced the Report of the New Ireland Forum in 1985 agreed that it was essential to involve unionists in the 'arrangements that would embody Irish unity' or in arrangements transitional to Irish unity. That is precisely what happened from the mid-19990s during the so-called 'peace process' that produced the Belfast Agreement. The involvement of the UUP/PUP/UDP leadership in the negotiations that led to the Belfast Agreement confirmed a core nationalist understanding of unionism. The SDLP and Sinn Fein/IRA understanding was that if 'Britain' and the Republic agreed the parameters of transitional arrangements for Irish unity and presented this as a *fait accompli* then unionists would participate in negotiating the detail of the outcome.

That is precisely what happened. The parameters of the transitional arrangements for Irish unity were agreed in the Downing Street Declaration of 15 December 1993 and in the Framework Document of 22 February 1995. The substantive content of the Belfast Agreement that the UUP/PUP/UDP negotiated was pre-determined in the Declaration and in the Framework Document. The UUP Referendum and Assembly election literature attempted to justify the UUP acceptance of the Agreement on the basis of claims about the Agreement that are mostly false. This obscures the real reason for the UUP acceptance of the Belfast Agreement. The real reason was the fear on the part of the UUP leadership that if the requirements of the Declaration and the Framework Document were not accepted they would in fact be imposed. The dominance of this thinking within the current UUP leadership was significantly reinforced by the influence of 'intellectuals' and academics whose

Capitulation to terror

political world is dominated by what they perceive to be 'nationalist realities' that they believe must be accommodated. The collapse of unionist self-confidence within the leadership of the UUP in the face of the *fait accompli* of the Downing Street Declaration and the Framework Document caused the UUP to negotiate and accept the transitional framework to Irish unity now established by the implementation of the Belfast Agreement. But all of this simply confirmed the SDLP and Sinn Fein/IRA understanding of how to gain unionist consent to the transitional mechanisms for Irish unity.

The Belfast Agreement and the corruption of democracy

The Agreement does not merely undermine the integrity of the Union. The Agreement is a radical corruption of democratic practice and the rule of law. The terms of the Belfast Agreement provide for members of Sinn Fein to govern the very citizens of Northern Ireland that the IRA terrorised. No price in terms of an authentic renunciation of violence was extracted by the UUP from Sinn Fein/IRA. The Agreement does not contain any requirement for the IRA to decommission its terrorist arsenal. The core section in the Agreement on decommissioning reads as follows:

> All participants accordingly affirm their commitment to the total disarmament of all paramilitary organisations. They also confirm their intention to continue to work constructively and in good faith with the Independent Commission, and to use any influence they may have to achieve the decommissioning of all paramilitary arms

within two years following endorsement in referendums North and South of the Agreement and in the context of the implementation of the overall settlement.

Contrary to the statements and handwritten pledges of the Prime Minister prior to the Referendum and the Assembly elections this section of the Agreement does not contain any requirement for the IRA to decommission as a condition of Sinn Fein taking seats in the Executive. This simply means that the statements by the Prime Minister were no more sophisticated or commendable than a pack of lies. But this was a politically significant 'pack of lies' because the Prime Minister's intervention undoubtedly prevented the collapse of the unionist 'Yes vote' during the week prior to the referendum.

Peace at any price

The section of the Agreement on decommissioning does not specifically differentiate Sinn Fein from the other political parties in terms of a responsibility for decommissioning. This in effect gives substance to the Sinn Fein/IRA claim that Sinn Fein is distinct from the IRA with no more responsibility for decommissioning than any other party to the Agreement. The section does not therefore contain any sanction against Sinn Fein in the event of the formation of an Executive and the refusal of the IRA to decommission. Sinn Fein, with the other political parties, is merely required to 'use any influence they may have to achieve the decommissioning of all paramilitary arms within two years'. This statement does not - contrary to frequent ill-informed media comment – contain a requirement for decommissioning to actually occur by May/June 2000. The refusal of the IRA to decommission by May/June 2000 could not, within the terms of the Agreement, be understood to indicate that Sinn Fein had failed 'to use any influence they may have' to bring about decommissioning by the IRA.

The simple fact of the matter is that the Agreement does not actually require decommissioning to occur. The Belfast Agreement clearly established the character of decommissioning as a 'voluntary act' (to use Peter Mandelson's terminology) and consequently established the legitimacy - within the terms of the Agreement - of the holding if not indeed the use of terrorist arms by the IRA and other terrorist organisations. This means that within the terms of the Agreement it is entirely acceptable for Sinn Fein to sit in the Executive backed by a fully-equipped terrorist 'murder machine'. The logic of these considerations is that the UUP negotiators accepted an Agreement that literally incorporates the Sinn Fein/IRA 'armalite and ballot box' strategy right into the heart of government in Northern Ireland.

But that did not prevent the leadership of the UUP from claiming in their Assembly election literature that in the Belfast Agreement the UUP had secured a requirement that 'for any terrorist group and/or its political wing' to hold ministerial office they must: declare that the war is over; end targeting, training, re-armament and punishment beatings; disband paramilitary structures; co-operate with the Independent Commission on Decommissioning; disarm within two years; disclose the fate of the 'disappeared' (*Ulster Unionist Voice*, June 1998). David Trimble formed the Executive (under the pretence that Seamus Mallon had not in fact previously retired on 15 July 1999 as Deputy First Minister) on 29 November 1999 without a single one of these requirements being met. These UUP commitments to the unionist electorate and the ease with which they were broken by the subsequent action by the UUP leadership in forming the Executive establish what decent people in Northern Ireland now clearly understand. The Belfast Agreement and the entire so-called 'peace process' is sustained by political mendacity on a staggering scale.

The UUP negotiated an agreement that provides for the wholesale release of terrorist prisoners by May/June 2000. The relevant section of the Belfast Agreement reads as follows:

> Both governments will put in place mechanisms to provide for an accelerated programme for the release of prisoners convicted of scheduled offences....Prisoners affiliated to organisations which have not established or are not maintaining a complete and unequivocal cease-fire will not benefit from the arrangements....In addition, the intention would be, that should circumstances

allow it, any qualifying prisoners who remained in custody two years after the commencement of the scheme would be released at that point.

This section of the Belfast Agreement means that all convicted terrorists (that is, individuals convicted of 'scheduled offences') who are 'affiliated with' terrorist organisations on 'cease-fire' will be out of prison by May/June 2000. This is a massive appeasement of terrorism. No demands are made on the terrorist organisations in terms even of an authentic cease-fire never mind in terms of an authentic renunciation of violence bearing in mind that a 'cease-fire' is not itself a renunciation of violence. To date 308 terrorist prisoners have been released. But what sorts of 'cease-fires' have existed in Northern Ireland since the signing of the Belfast Agreement on 10 April 1998. The following statistics are available from the reports of the Police Authority for Northern Ireland.

Number of deaths due to security situation

	1996	1997	1998	1999
RUC	0	3	1	0
RUCR	0	1	0	0
Army	1	1	1	0
UDR/RIR	0	0	0	0
Civilian	14	17	52	7

Security incidents

	1996	1997	1998	1999
Shootings	25	225	175	125*
Bombings	4	93	123	82*
Incendiaries	0	9	20	7*

* provisional figures

Despite this appalling catalogue of 'republican' and 'loyalist' murder and barbarity (which does not include the statistics of beatings and mutilation and exile carried out by the paramilitary groups) Mo Mowlam ruled on 27 August 1999 that the IRA cease-fire was intact. The murder of Charles Bennett on 29 July 1999 by the IRA and the importation of arms by the IRA from the United States during the summer of 1999 were the occasion of this ruling by the Secretary of State. The Secretary of State conceded that the involvement of the IRA in the murder of Charles Bennett and in the importation of arms from the United States was beyond doubt. Nevertheless the Secretary of State ruled on the grounds of 'all the factors specified' in the 1998 Northern Ireland (Sentences) Act that there was 'an insufficient basis to conclude that the IRA cease-fire had broken down'.

The ruling was subsequently upheld by the Northern Ireland High Court on 19 November 1999 in the face of a legal challenge from Michelle Williamson. The objective of Michelle Williamson's challenge was to stop the release of terrorist prisoners and in particular the release of Sean Kelly convicted on 27 January 1995 for his part in the Shankill bomb of 23 October 1993. The Shankill bomb killed two children and ten adults including Michelle Williamson's mother and father.

The Belfast Agreement and the 1998 Northern Ireland (Sentences) Act require a 'complete and unequivocal cease-fire' as the condition for the 'accelerated release' of terrorist prisoners. Mr Justice Kerr rejected Michelle Williamson's legal challenge in the High Court on 19 November 1999. Mr Justice Kerr ruled that even if the Secretary of State concluded that 'the relevant organisation had failed to fulfill any of the criteria provided for it was still open to her to conclude that the organisation was maintaining a complete and unequivocal cease-fire' (*Irish Independent*, 20 November 1999).

This judgment means that the determination of a 'complete and unequivocal cease-fire' is entirely at the discretion of the Secretary of State. The fact of the matter is that at the time of the Secretary of State's judgment the IRA was not complying with any of the requirements set out in Section 9 of the Sentences Act for a 'complete and unequivocal cease-fire'. Mo Mowlam's decision on 27 August 1999 established that murder and the procuring of arms (despite the assurances by the Prime Minister in July 1999, backed by the International Body on Decommissioning, that there had been a 'seismic shift' on the part of Sinn Fein/IRA in the direction of decommissioning) were not breaches of a 'complete and unequivocal cease-fire'. These considerations simply mean that the term 'complete and unequivocal cease-fire' is nothing more than a verbal sleight of hand that imposes no real constraint on the terrorist activity of the IRA or any other terrorist group.

This makes it difficult to avoid the conclusion that the legislative sovereignty of Parliament is now being used to legally undermine the integrity of the rule of law in the United Kingdom. The requirements of the Belfast Agreement on the 'accelerated release' of terrorist prisoners were given legal effect by the 1998 Northern Ireland (Sentences) Act. The Act was passed in Westminster not on the strength of the government's majority but with the approval of virtually the entire House of Commons. The Act applies only to prisoners who have committed a 'scheduled offence' which is legal jargon for a terrorist offence. But to make imprisonment for a terrorist offence a necessary condition in law for 'accelerated release' from prison is to come as near to legitimising the terrorist offence as makes no difference.

Further, the Act does not require the 'scheduled offender' to renounce membership of the terrorist organisation to which he/she belonged at the time of the offence. The Act requires that the terrorist organisation to which the 'scheduled offender' is 'affiliated' (to use the terminology of the Belfast Agreement) must 'establish' and 'maintain' a 'complete and unequivocal cease-fire'. But in any legal system based on respect for the integrity of the rule of law the fact of being 'affiliated' with a criminal and terrorist organisation would never be regarded as the extenuating or mitigating basis for an 'accelerated release' from prison. This consideration is strengthened by the fact that the High Court ruling against Michelle Williamson established that the term 'complete and unequivocal cease-fire' has no determinate content other than that supplied by a Secretary of State politically fixated with the appeasement of Sinn Fein/IRA.

These considerations simply mean that the Sentences Act is a legalised corruption of the rule of law. This corruption of the rule of law was subsequently repeated in the Northern Ireland (Location of Victims Remains) Act passed by Parliament on 12 May 1999 with 324 votes for and 5 votes against the Act. This Act prohibits the admissibility in criminal proceedings of information resulting from the recovery of the remains of people abducted and murdered by the IRA (the 'disappeared') except when such evidence is 'adduced on behalf of the accused'. The Location of Victims Remains Act is in effect a legalised obstruction of justice literally dictated to Parliament by the IRA as the condition for disclosing information (which was entirely inadequate if not deliberately misleading) about the location of the graves of these IRA victims.

The legitimisation of this legalised corruption of the rule of law goes back to the Mitchell Report of 22 January 1996. The Report recommended that in the event of decommissioning (which was not actually required by the Report) the terrorist weapons should be exempt from forensic testing and that information resulting from decommissioning should be inadmissible as evidence in courts of law in the United Kingdom and in the Republic. These recommendations of the Mitchell Report were incorporated into the Northern Ireland Decommissioning Act of 27 February 1997 by the Parliament of the United Kingdom. The legislation that underpins the implementation of the Belfast Agreement is an affront to justice and to common decency. The 'Mother of Parliaments' has been contaminated by the appeasement of terrorism and by subservience to the Irish nationalist caucus that directs the Northern Ireland policy of the Clinton administration.

The Belfast Agreement and the destruction of the RUC

The implementation of the Belfast Agreement has resulted in the legalised corruption of the rule of law. The public morality required to sustain the rule of law has been replaced in Parliament by an expediency that places no constraint on the appeasement of terrorism. But these considerations do not nearly exhaust the extent of the appeasement of terrorism within the Belfast Agreement. Jack Holland in his recently published *Hope Against History* develops the central thesis of the book that by 1994 the IRA was facing defeat. This was primarily the work of the RUC/RUCR but at enormous cost in terms of the murder and injury of RUC/RUCR officers as a result of IRA and other 'republican' terrorism.

Nevertheless the destruction of the RUC/RUCR is a core requirement of the Belfast Agreement. The Belfast Agreement requires a 'new beginning to policing in Northern Ireland'. This requirement is based on the understanding on the part of those who negotiated the Belfast Agreement that:

> It is essential that policing structures and arrangements are such that the police service is professional, effective and efficient, fair and impartial, free from partisan political control; accountable, both under the law for its actions and to the community it serves; representative of the society it polices, and operates within a coherent and co-operative criminal system, which conforms with human rights norms.

This section of the Agreement is a radical denigration of the operational efficiency, legal accountability and professional integrity of the entire RUC. The negotiators of the Belfast Agreement obviously considered that the RUC was so deficient in terms of these requirements that 'a new beginning to policing' was imperative for Northern Ireland. The Patten Report incorporates the letter and spirit of this section of the Belfast Agreement. In short, the Patten Report is a blueprint for the destruction of the RUC.

The content of the Patten Report - in keeping with the terms of reference for the Patten Commission in the Agreement - is determined by a fundamental perspective set out in paragraph 1.9. This paragraph states that the so-called 'reform' of policing in Northern Ireland 'should not be a cluster of unconnected adjustments...that can be bolted or soldered onto the organisation that already exists'. The 'organisation that already exists' is the RUC. This means that the fundamental perspective of the Patten Report is that the implementation of the recommendations of the Report is entirely incompatible with the continued existence of the RUC. The Secretary of State set out the commitment of the government to the full implementation of the Patten Report in a statement to the House of Commons on 19 January 2000. The new so-called 'police service' for Northern Ireland recommended in the Patten Report will be radically different from the RUC in terms of symbolic identity, basis of allegiance, organisational structure and (over a relatively short period of time) personnel. Not even the name will remain.

The imperative of the Patten Report to destroy the RUC is based on an unbelievable inversion of reality. For the members of the Patten Commission, terrorism is not central to the intractability of political conflict in Northern Ireland. The Patten Report makes the RUC the cause of the persistence of political instability and terrorism in Northern Ireland. The Patten Report presents the RUC as being at the 'heart of...the problems that politicians have been unable to resolve in Northern Ireland'. The logic of the Report is that

Doing the IRA's work

the effective destruction of the RUC must be central to a process that the Report claims is required to restore the 'values of liberty, the rule of law and mutual respect' and to 'reorient policing in Northern Ireland onto an approach based on upholding human rights and respecting human dignity'.

The authors of the Report obviously considered that these values are absent from policing in Northern Ireland and that the restoration and maintenance of these values is incompatible with the continued existence of the RUC. The Report explicitly states that 'by means of a fresh start for policing, our aim is to help ensure that past tragedies are not repeated in the future'. The clear implication of this statement is that the destruction of the RUC is required to prevent a repetition of the 'tragedies of the past'. This means that the RUC must - in the mind of the authors of the Patten Report - have been in some unspecified way responsible for these 'tragedies'. This is a gross and offensive insult to the memory of the RUC/RUCR officers who were murdered (302) and maimed (nearly 10,000) in defence of liberty and the rule of law against the onslaught of thirty years of Sinn Fein/IRA terrorism.

In keeping with this inversion of reality the Patten Report deploys a tactic of 'demonisation' against the RUC. This is a tactic that has been central to Sinn Fein/IRA and SDLP strategy for thirty years. The tactic involves the relentless propagation of a propaganda of denigration. What is the political motivation that lies behind this tactic of 'demonisation'? The political motivation is to remove every security barrier to the SDLP and Sinn Fein/IRA goal of the political unification of the island of Ireland. The nationalist historian Tim Pat Coogan in *The IRA* stated that 'the B-Specials were the rock on which any mass movement by the IRA in the North inevitably foundered' The same judgment could be extended to the Ulster Defence Regiment (UDR). The UDR was a rock of resistance against the terrorism of the IRA. Both were destroyed by the nationalist tactic of 'demonisation'. The RUC has held the front line against terrorism since the mid-1970s. The RUC developed an internationally respected counter-terrorist expertise capable not merely of sustaining the fight against the IRA but of actually defeating the IRA. This is the explanation of a core pan-nationalist strategy, based on agreement between Hume and Adams, to destroy the RUC.

This Sinn Fein/IRA and SDLP strategy of 'demonisation' directed against the RUC has the unqualified support of the Clinton administration and the US House of Representatives. For example, on 22 July 1999 the House of Representatives unanimously accepted a report on the RUC by the Committee on International Relations. The RUC is presented in the Report as 'the enforcement arm of the dominant unionist majority' and as a 'Gestapo-type organisation' which is 'rotten to its core'. Both the Sinn Fein/IRA and the SDLP propaganda against the RUC fed these outrageous sentiments. Mr Mallon is a vociferous anti-RUC propagandist. For example, at the Brehon Law Society 'Irishman of the Year' award in Philadelphia on 24 April 1999, the then Deputy First Minister (Designate) took the opportunity to inform his United States audience that in 'the North of Ireland' the rule of law has been reduced by the RUC to 'little more than the rule of the jungle'. This is precisely the understanding of the role of the RUC that determined the conclusion of the Report by the House of Representatives Committee on International Relations. The Report concluded that 'the RUC had been at the very core of – indeed had given rise to – the human rights abuses and civil unrest that have plagued Northern Ireland for the last thirty years'.

The position of the Committee on International Relations is that terrorism in Northern Ireland is not driven by Sinn Fein/IRA but by the RUC. But this perversion of reality is not confined to the rigid and ignorant nationalism that directs the policy of the Clinton administration on Northern Ireland. The Patten Report fully incorporates this entire mind-set. The core logic of the Patten Report is that what the Report refers to as the 'return of hope, healing and peace' to Northern Ireland requires the effective destruction of the RUC and the incorporation of 'republicans' (to use the precise language of the Report) into a new so-called Northern Ireland 'police service'.

The case made in the Patten Report for the destruction of the RUC is entirely without foundation. The Patten Report itself had to acknowledge that the RUC had the highest rating in western Europe in terms of public satisfaction with police performance against crime. This comparative RUC rating for western Europe, contained in the International Victimisation Survey for 1997, is entirely in keeping with the results of annual Community Attitude Surveys in Northern Ireland. The average findings of the Community Attitude Surveys over a number of years show that 66% of Catholics and 73% of Protestants considered that the RUC dealt 'efficiently' with 'ordinary crime' and 65% of Catholics and 87% of Protestants considered that the RUC dealt 'fairly with everyone when combating terrorist and sectarian crime'. On the issue of recruitment to the RUC 74% of Catholics gave 'fear of intimidation or attack on them or their relatives' as what deters Catholics from joining the RUC. These Community Attitude Survey findings show a high level of acceptability of the RUC in combating both terrorist and non-terrorist crime. The fact of the matter is that nationalist propaganda and intimidation failed to alienate the majority of the Catholic community in Northern Ireland from the RUC. This is a remarkable achievement for the RUC given the political nature of terrorism in Northern Ireland and the dual role of the RUC in civilian policing and counter-terrorism.

Why are these statistics important? The statistics are important because they conclusively refute a core claim in the Patten Report. The claim is that as far as the RUC is concerned 'the consent required right across the community in any liberal democracy for effective policing has been absent' This claim is the ostensible basis for the effective destruction of the RUC recommended in the Patten Report. The claim in the Report that the RUC lacks the consent required for effective policing is demonstrably false. The reality is that the statistics used by the Report itself almost certainly demonstrate a level of cross community support for the RUC that would not be matched by any other police force in the United Kingdom.

So what is the real reason for the effective destruction of the RUC? The real reason is that the destruction of the RUC is a core demand of Sinn Fein/IRA backed by the SDLP. Sinn Fein/IRA know that without the destruction of the RUC the terrorist war cannot be won. The SDLP position is equally tied into the demands and objectives of Irish nationalism and is set out in a 1995 SDLP policy document, *Policing in Northern Ireland.* This SDLP policy document claims that what it calls the 'problem of policing in Northern Ireland' is 'incapable of resolution' in the absence of a so-called 'political settlement' agreeable to nationalists. The SDLP objection to the RUC is fundamentally a political objection which the SDLP shares with Sinn Fein/IRA and which is based on the demands of Irish nationalism. This means that no amount of so-called 'reform' of the RUC would make the RUC acceptable to the SDLP. The real strategy of the SDLP is to utilise a concocted claim that the RUC is radically unacceptable to Catholics as a powerful lever for constitutional change in Northern Ireland in the direction of Irish unity.

The Patten Report meets the core requirement of Sinn Fein/IRA and the SDLP for the destruction of the RUC. But that is not the final appeasement of terrorism within the Report. The Patten Report recommends the replacement of the RUC with a Northern Ireland Police Service (NIPS). This designation was changed by the Secretary of State to the Police Service for Northern Ireland (PSNI). Sinn Fein/IRA is guaranteed a central role in the political control and operational structure of the new so-called 'police dispensation' in Northern Ireland. Recruitment from the 'republican movement' is a reiterated requirement of the Report. The Report states that 'the police service in Northern Ireland needs to include appropriately large numbers of nationalists, **including republicans,** if it is to be fully effective'. The inclusion of republicans (that is, individuals committed to IRA terrorism) in policing in Northern Ireland will also be accommodated by the recommendation of the Report that so-called 'police support services' should be 'contracted out' by district councils and paid for out of local rates. There is absolutely no doubt that in nationalist controlled districts in Northern Ireland these so-called 'police support services' will be provided by the membership of the IRA.

The incorporation of Sinn Fein/IRA into the very heart of policing in Northern Ireland is located within the Report in an all-Ireland framework. The Patten Report clearly envisages the development of an all-Ireland

Replacing the RUC

police structure. This all-Ireland police structure will **initially** be based on the recruitment of members of the Garda Siochana into the PSNI and on a programme of 'long-term personnel exchanges...between the Northern Ireland police and the Garda'. The location of the new Northern Ireland 'police service' within an all-Ireland structure of policing will provide a developing role for the Republic in the policing of Northern Ireland. These all-Ireland structures of policing will be developed within the remit of the Intergovernmental Conference over which the Executive and the Assembly have no control.

The Republic, to which the Patten Report gives this developing role in policing in Northern Ireland, has effectively been a 'safe haven' for the IRA and other republican terrorists since 1970. Members of Jack Lynch's Fianna Fail government established the Provisional IRA in the early 1970s. The role of the Fianna Fail party in setting up the Provisional IRA was clearly outlined by Conor Cruise O'Brien in his introduction to Martin Dillon's book, *The Dirty War:*

> The deal that launched the Provos was essentially this: certain members of the Lynch government approached those leading members of the IRA who were known to be disgusted with the Marxist leadership, on both nationalist and Catholic grounds, and also on operational grounds. These leaders - who were to become the leaders of the Provisional IRA - were offered money, arms and general support if they would abjure operations against the Republic, and concentrate on operations inside Northern Ireland. The Provisional leaders to be agreed. The new policy, in exchange for which the emerging Provos received support from the then Dublin government, is enshrined in the IRA's General Orders No. 8, which is still in force and is set out in the IRA's Green Book..... Thus the Provos were born and the dirty war began.

The relevant section of the IRA General Army Order reads as follows:

> Volunteers are strictly forbidden to take any military action against 26 County forces under any circumstances whatsoever. The

importance of this order in present circumstances especially in the border areas cannot be over-emphasised.

The status of the Republic as a 'safe haven' for republican terrorists is beyond dispute due to the maintenance of a Sinn Fein/IRA headquarters in Dublin; the failure of successive governments in the Republic over a thirty year period to extradite republican terrorists to the jurisdiction of the United Kingdom; and the storage and ease of movement of a huge arsenal of IRA arms in the Republic. These considerations mean that the Republic of Ireland has been responsible over a period of thirty years for what is in effect state-sponsored terrorism directed against the Protestant and unionist community in Northern Ireland.

The implementation of the Report will establish the policing of law-abiding citizens in Northern Ireland by IRA terrorists within a developing all-Ireland structure involving the country (the Republic) that initiated and sustained IRA terrorism in Northern Ireland. The Patten Report rewards thirty years of Sinn Fein/IRA terrorism by incorporating both the terrorists and the state (the Republic) that sponsored them into the policing of the society against which that terrorism was directed. The *Daily Telegraph* of 28 September, 1999 described this scenario as an 'insane project'. That is true but not the whole truth. The implementation of the Patten Report will destroy the rule of law in Northern Ireland that the officers of the RUC fought and died to defend and incorporate the terrorist organisation responsible for their murder into the policing of Northern Ireland. The truth is that the Patten Report exemplifies not mere insanity but wickedness on any civilised understanding of the requirements of public morality.

Finally, every single one of these recommendations of the Patten Report is in keeping with the requirements of the Belfast Agreement. The Agreement requires that the new so-called 'police service' must 'recognise the full and equal legitimacy and worth of the identities, senses of allegiance and ethos of all sections of the community in Northern Ireland'. This means that the Agreement requires that policing in Northern Ireland must be based on a recognition of the 'legitimacy and worth' of the Irish republican tradition that spawned and has sustained thirty years of IRA terrorism in Northern Ireland. That is the precise content of the Belfast Agreement that the UUP leadership delivered on 10 April 1998. But this did not deter the UUP leadership from insulting the intelligence of the unionist electorate by claiming at the time of the Referendum and the Assembly election that the Belfast Agreement had 'saved' the RUC. The fact that the UUP leadership made this claim means that the UUP leadership is either devoid of political integrity or they simply did not understand the content of the Belfast Agreement that they actually negotiated. The decision by the Secretary of State to implement the Patten Report in full has put Mr Trimble in the position where he has only one honourable option and that is to resign as First Minister and collapse the Executive.

The Belfast Agreement and the legitimisation of Sinn Fein/ IRA terrorism

The implementation of the Belfast Agreement has given rise to a staggering appeasement of the terrorism of Sinn Fein/IRA. The Agreement permits the inclusion of Sinn Fein in the Executive without any requirement for the decommissioning of the terrorist arsenals. That is precisely what happened when Mr Trimble agreed to the formation of the Executive on 2 December 1999 without the IRA decommissioning a single bullet. This was a direct repudiation of the UUP pledge in the election to the European parliament on 10 June 1999 that 'the Party reaffirms its manifesto pledge that we will not sit in an Executive with Sinn Fein until the IRA has begun a credible, verifiable and ongoing process of decommissioning leading to complete disarmament by May 2000'. The formation of the Executive on 2 December 1999 fully incorporated the threat of terrorism into the government of Northern Ireland. The outcome of the Mitchell Review in November 1999 has in fact fully legitimised this state of affairs because the Mitchell

Review established that decommissioning (if it ever occurs) must be a 'voluntary' act on the part of the terrorist organisations. This has been fully endorsed by the government of the United Kingdom in numerous comments by the Secretary of State on the Mitchell Review.

This state of affairs is absolutely incompatible with democracy. The core of democracy consists in the requirement that the conduct of politics must be free from the threat or use of violence. Democratic government must be based entirely on electoral support. This means that no political party in a democracy can claim a right to be involved in government on the basis of a so-called 'electoral mandate' while at the same time retaining at its disposal the persuasion that comes from the barrel of a gun. The implementation of the Belfast Agreement has in fact incorporated into the government of Northern Ireland the Sinn Fein/IRA combination of the 'armalite and the ballot box'. This is entirely incompatible with the primary duty of government to protect citizens from violence or the threat of violence. The citizens of Northern Ireland are now in effect governed not on the basis of a respect for the requirements of democracy and the rule of law but on the basis of nothing more commendable than the terrorist imperatives of the strategic thinking of Sinn Fein/IRA.

The support given to the Belfast Agreement by the nationalist electorate in Northern Ireland clearly demonstrates that the appeasement of Sinn Fein/IRA terrorism to the extent required by the Belfast Agreement is not morally or politically problematic for this electorate. But the appeasement of terrorism required by the Belfast Agreement has split the unionist electorate. The government anticipated this. Prior to the 1998 Referendum the NIO Director of Communications prepared an extensive propaganda strategy document for Mo Mowlam. The objective of this strategy document was to 'sell' the Agreement to the unionist electorate at the time of the Referendum by exploiting the 'public's desire for peace'. This document focused significantly on the propaganda value of the support of the business and church leaders, which was in fact taken for granted in the document. The relevant section of the so-called 'information strategy' document read as follows:

> Each focus group should be representative of a section of the wider community. Those wider groups in turn each have someone they look up to as a representative figure. We should where possible be enlisting the help of those people to champion our cause, for example, ...the church leaders, the heads of community organisations and trade unions, and other members of the G7. While any overt manipulation could only be counter-productive, a carefully co-ordinated timetable of statements from these people will be helpful in giving our message credibility with those they represent. It has the added benefit of providing a fresh face for that message, and ensuring that it is not only the government which is seen to be selling the process.

The support given to the Belfast Agreement by the self-styled Group of Seven (G7) business and trade union leaders has the merit of simplicity. Basically, the G7 message is that 'peace' is an absolute requirement for the economic 'regeneration' of Northern Ireland. But simplicity is the only merit of this message. The subtext of the G7 position is that whatever appeasement of terrorism is required to secure 'peace' is acceptable to the business community. The problem with the G7 position is that it isolates the understanding of the requirements for economic development from any real commitment to democratic practice or respect for the rule of law. This means that the G7 members consider that economic 'regeneration' can occur in tandem with putting into effect a political agreement that contains a blueprint for the extensive criminalisation of government and indeed for the criminalisation of the economic life of Northern Ireland.

The historian, Andrew Roberts, has perceptively remarked that:

> In business matters, individual businessmen may display great sagacity (somewhat lacking in our local variety) but when they collectively pronounce on politics they have long tended to display astonishing myopia and stupidity. No public body was keener on the appeasement of Nazi Germany that the CBI's predecessor, the British Federation of Industry.

Roberts was commenting on the involvement of British business organisations in the appeasement of nazism in the late 1930s. Roberts' comments are entirely appropriate for the involvement of the local business and trade union leaders in the appeasement of the terrorism of Sinn Fein/IRA required by the Belfast Agreement.

The major churches in Northern Ireland are champions of the Belfast Agreement. The type of thinking that has formed the response of the clerical ideologues of the Agreement across the denominations is exemplified in the statements of the self-styled Evangelical Contribution on Northern Ireland (ECONI).

The ECONI statements are responses by that organisation to crucial moments in the so-called 'peace process' prior to the Referendum (particularly the Downing Street Declaration and the IRA 'cease-fires') and to issues arising out of the implementation of the Belfast Agreement - for example, the release of terrorist prisoners and the outcome of the Mitchell Review in November 1999.

Each statement could be read with considerable justification as an unconnected series of sanctimonious platitudes and Biblical quotations. But beneath the appearance (and at times reality) of incoherence there is a discernable pattern of thought. This pattern of thought is perhaps most readily detectable in the ECONI statement on Mo Mowlam's ruling on the state of the IRA cease-fire on 26 August 1999. This ECONI statement develops in a few lines a focus on what ECONI presents as an unavoidable tension in the life of the Christian. The Christian is a member of the 'church' or 'Kingdom of God'. The life of the church involves commitment to the 'ideal of a society shaped and governed by principle'. But the Christian is also a 'citizen' and a member of 'society'. The ECONI understanding is that the corrupt character of 'society' renders 'pragmatism' (understood as a modification or departure from strict adherence to principle) unavoidable for the Christian. The ECONI position is that 'in a fallen world at times we have to lower our expectations and deal with political realities' and that 'in the interaction and confrontation between these two communities - church and society - there will always be tension and ambiguity'.

The ECONI statements on the 'peace process' and on the implementation of the Belfast Agreement fall into two distinct groups. There are statements in which the ECONI position is based on appeal to the 'values of the Kingdom'. This was the basis of the ECONI response to the Downing Street Declaration. The Downing Street Declaration of 15 December 1993 conceded the fundamental principle of Irish nationalism that there is a single nation or 'people' on the island of Ireland with a 'right of self-determination'. This means that the Declaration undermined the legitimacy of unionism. The ECONI response was a tacit recommendation (never explicitly stated) to accept the Declaration. Rejection of the Declaration was identified in the ECONI statement with commitment to the ideology of 'For God and Ulster' which was set out as incompatible with the absolute imperatives of the 'values of the Kingdom'.

This is a standard ECONI response to a commitment to unionism. The 'trick' is to tacitly or implicitly (so that it is always possible for ECONI spokespersons to retreat under pressure of counter-argument) align a commitment to unionism with a subordination of the 'values of the Kingdom' to the values of 'politics', 'culture' or 'nation'. The fact of the matter is that no such subordination is required by a commitment to unionism. Unionism involves nothing more than a commitment to the 'cherished position of equal citizenship within the United Kingdom'. Unionism is therefore entirely compatible with authentic Christian allegiance to God. The ECONI statements on issues central to unionism (such as the Downing Street Declaration) amount to a subtle use of theological rhetoric to attempt to immobilise unionist opposition to the accommodation of the political demands of Irish nationalism.

But on issues relating to the accommodation or appeasement of IRA terrorism in the 'peace process' and in the implementation of the Belfast Agreement the ECONI statements are dominantly based on an appeal to pragmatism. This appeal to pragmatism is particularly clear in the ECONI statements on the issue of the release of terrorist prisoners and on Mo Mowlam's ruling on the state of the IRA cease-fire. The ECONI position on these two issues is set out as follows:

> While the Belfast Agreement required the setting aside of one aspect of the system of justice (keeping terrorists in prison), the goal of this was the creation of a just and peaceful society for all. On this basis Christians were able with a good conscience to accept that the strict demands of justice could be set aside for the sake of the wider goal of a just and peaceful society. It is on the same basis that Christians can with a good conscience accept that parties linked to paramilitary groups who have violated cease-fires and attacked the principle of peaceful politics can remain within the process. They have their place, not by moral right, but in the interests of the wider hope of peace and justice for the community.

The argument here, in concrete terms, is that the pursuit of 'peace and justice for the community' means that 'Christians' can 'with a good conscience' accept the release of terrorist prisoners and the inclusion, in the government of Northern Ireland, of the representatives of terrorist organisations that murder with impunity. This argument is a perversion of common decency larded over with the theological rhetoric of 'risk-taking' based on 'hope in God' and demanded by ECONI of 'Christians' in order to emulate the 'radical, vulnerable, risk-taking Jesus'. The ECONI statements exemplify the moral dangers of superficial theology obscured by the tone of superior self-righteousness that permeates the ECONI statements.The problem with the ECONI recom-

The clergy's choice

mendations to 'Christians' is that they are almost entirely divorced from a clear understanding of the public moral-ity required by the Christian tradition for the conduct of gov-ernment. Put briefly, this public morality imposes on government the fundamental duty to protect the innocent and to punish the wrong-doer. There is no room in the public morality of the Christian tradition for the appeasement of the Sinn Fein/IRA ideology of terror.

The unionist electorate has resisted the moral intimidation of church leaders and religious organisations such as ECONI. The 1998 Assembly election produced a clear majority of first preference votes for unionist parties (DUP, UKUP, Independent Unionists and the Northern Ireland Conservative Party) opposed to the Belfast Agreement.

Pro-Agreement and Anti-Agreement First Preference Unionist Votes in the Assembly Election

Anti-Agreement Votes		Pro-Agreement Votes	
DUP	146,989	UUP	172,225
UKUP	36,541	PUP	20,634
Independent Unionists	23,127	UDP	8,651
Conservative Party	1,835		
Total	**208,492**		**201,510**

The MRNI opinion poll published on 26 October 1999 showed a virtual collapse in support for the Belfast Agreement among Protestant voters and specifically among the UUP electorate.

Referendum Vote for the Belfast Agreement

		May 1998[■]	October 1999[♦]
Protestant	Yes	64	49
	No	36	51
Catholic	Yes	89	88
	No	11	12
Ulster Unionist	Yes	82	56
Party	No	18	44

[■] Answer to the question 'how you voted in the Referendum for the Belfast Agreement'.

[♦] Answer to the question 'if the Referendum was held today how would you vote'.

The growing antipathy of the unionist electorate to the Belfast Agreement is due to at least two considerations. First, the outworking of the Agreement - the release of terrorist prisoners, the formation of the Executive including Sinn Fein without IRA decommissioning, and the Patton Report - has concretely displayed the true character of the Belfast Agreement as a affront to common decency. Second, a number of victims' organisations have been formed since the signing of the Belfast Agreement – organisations such as FAIR, FACT, GIVE, FEAR, HAVEN, HURT, HOPE, West Tyrone Voice and South Down Action Healing Wounds. The people who belong to these organisations are, in the most authentic sense of the term, 'innocent victims' of terrorism. Each one of them has experienced the loss of loved ones murdered by the IRA or by other republican terrorists.

Forgotten victims

The victims' organisations have powerfully focused public awareness on the shattering impact of terrorism on the lives of innocent citizens. This has coincided with the actual legitimisation of terrorism which is required by the terms of the Belfast Agreement and which has been put into effect by the implementation of the Agreement. The result has been a heightened understanding within the unionist community of the extent to which the Belfast Agreement is a straightforward accommodation of the evil of terrorism. The growing antagonism of the unionist electorate to the Belfast Agreement is testimony to the sense of moral propriety that exists within unionism and which also caused the unionist electorate to dismiss the UDP and give a derisory vote to the PUP in the 1998 Assembly elections.

The opposition to the Belfast Agreement must be consolidated and directed at the level of political leadership in Northern Ireland. This is an urgent task. The architects of the Belfast Agreement calculated that the Trimble leadership would have sufficient support within the UUP to drive the crucial initial stages of implementation. To date that calculation has proved to be correct. Union First and the UUP Westminster MPs opposed to the Belfast Agreement do not effectively control the UUP. The DUP and the three members of the United Unionist Party opted on 2 December 1999 to participate in the Executive and its statutory committees without decommissioning (or any likelihood of decommissioning) on the part of the IRA. Participation in the structures of government - the Executive and its statutory committees - established under the Agreement is not compatible with effective and authentic opposition to the implementation of the Belfast Agreement. These considerations clearly demonstrate that the coherent political leadership that is required to effectively direct unionist opposition to the Belfast Agreement does not at the present time exist.

This is precisely the situation that the architects of the Belfast Agreement require in order to proceed with the consolidation of the implementation of the Agreement. The game-plan of the Belfast Agreement is to put into operation the institutions of an all-Ireland state. The effective working of these institutions will require the transformation of the political culture of Northern Ireland to accommodate Irish unity. This transformation of political culture will therefore crucially involve the erosion of a commitment to unionism within Northern Ireland.

The education system is obviously central to the project of the cultural transformation required in Northern Ireland to consolidate the core objectives of the Belfast Agreement. The blueprint for the central involvement of the education system in Northern Ireland in this transformation of political culture is contained in *Towards a Culture of Tolerance: Education for Diversity*, issued by the Department of Education (DENI) in September 1999. This is the Report of the Working Group on the Strategic Promotion of Education for Mutual Understanding. This group was established by DENI in June 1998 immediately following the referendum on the Belfast Agreement. The terms of reference for the Working Group were based on the understanding that the Belfast Agreement has 'created a new opportunity to reflect afresh on the role of education as a source of social cohesion within Northern Ireland'.

The core recommendation of the Report is that the 'promotion of tolerance and reconciliation' in Northern Ireland must be the 'seminal purpose' of what the Report calls the 'Northern Ireland Education Service'. The Report states that:

> The Belfast Agreement represents an attempt to establish new democratic structures in Northern Ireland to replace the 'culture of violence'...The success of new democratic structures will be dependent on the extent to which they contribute to the development of a fair and just society, based on respect for diversity. While it is self-evident that education alone cannot guarantee these outcomes - this is a task shared by the whole community - nevertheless education has a seminal role in laying the foundations.

Martin McGuinness as the new Minister for Education will have the responsibility for ensuring that the education system is effectively used to consolidate the implementation of the Belfast Agreement. The central perspective of the Report is that the effective operation of the 'new democratic structures in Northern Ireland' will require a social transformation from what the Report calls a 'culture of violence' to a 'culture of tolerance'. But this central perspective of the Report demonstrates that the Report is itself nothing more than an exercise in nationalist propaganda.

There are two reasons for this conclusion. First, the Belfast Agreement incorporates IRA terrorism into the heart of government in Northern Ireland. The Agreement is therefore, contrary to the presentation in the Report, a radical corruption of democracy. Second, the Report is based on the nationalist understanding that terrorism in Northern Ireland was due to a pervasive 'culture of violence'. What is a 'culture of violence'? The term 'culture of violence' refers to dispositions, beliefs and practices that the authors of the Report consider give rise to violence and in the case of Northern Ireland to terrorism. But the statistics of terrorism in Northern Ireland set out in *Lost Lives* clearly demonstrate that terrorism was driven by the IRA and other republican terrorist groups. This is not to minimise the savagery of so-called 'loyalist' terrorism. These considerations mean that the logic of the Report is that the terrorism of the IRA and other republican groups was the outcome of a pervasive 'culture of violence' in Northern Ireland.

The 'culture of violence' in Northern Ireland was, according to the Report, marked by a pervasive opposition to (not mere absence of) 'pluralism', 'social justice', 'human rights', and 'democratic freedom'.

These ideals are never fully adhered to in any society. This means that a case can always be made for their more extensive implementation and Northern Ireland is no exception. But that is not the argument of the Report. The argument of the Report is that these values were so pervasively absent in Northern Ireland as to actually produce thirty years of terrorism. This argument amounts to nothing more sophisticated than a regurgitation of nationalist propaganda used to legitimise thirty years of Sinn Fein/IRA terrorism. The central recommendation of the Report is that this nationalist propaganda should be 'mainstreamed' into the educational curriculum to provide 'political education' in 'understanding conflict'.

IRA terrorism was (and is) sustained by a 'culture of violence' - but it is a culture of violence that is at the heart of Irish nationalism. The decades of murder and destruction in Northern Ireland have been primarily due to the fanaticism and savagery of so-called 'Irish republicanism'. The fanaticism and savagery of Sinn Fein/IRA is rooted in a carefully fostered canon of Irish history that has transmitted a powerful sense of historical grievance. This sense of historical grievance was directed after 1920 against the unionist and Protestant community in Northern Ireland. The deep-rooted sense of historical grievance that focused on Stormont after 1920 was reinforced by an imagined sense of systematic oppression and discrimination. For example, the historian A.T.Q. Stewart in *The Narrow Ground* describes the northern nationalist self-understanding as 'a picture of unrelieved blackness, of a people grievously oppressed and denied any means of redress'.

The 1984 *Report of the New Ireland Forum* presented the understanding that Partition had established a 'system of exclusively unionist power and privilege' within which a 'unionist supremacy' exercised 'untrammeled rule' against a minority suffering 'systematic discrimination' and 'deprived of the means of social and economic development'. The *Report of the New Ireland Forum* produced no evidence to substantiate these claims. That is not surprising because these claims are entirely without foundation. The nationalist experience in Northern Ireland was not one of systematic discrimination and oppression. The chapter on the issue of discrimination in Northern Ireland by Graham Gudgin in the recently published book, *The Northern Ireland Question: Nationalism, Unionism and Partition*, edited by P.J.Roche and Brian Barton, is a powerful challenge to this nationalist orthodoxy.

The self-perception of northern nationalists that they are an 'oppressed people' may be understood to be an expression of what the historian Liam Kennedy in *Colonialism, Religion and Nationalism in Ireland* has described as 'a syndrome of attitudes that might be summed up by the acronym MOPE, that is, the most oppressed people ever'. This historical self-delusion has maintained a mind-set that gave rise to the conditions in which the mobilisation strategies of the Provisional IRA were able to effectively sustain thirty years of unmitigated barbarity in Northern Ireland. But what *Towards a Culture of Tolerance: Education for Diversity in Northern Ireland* is effectively recommending is that this nationalist orthodoxy - the propaganda of MOPE - should be 'mainstreamed' into the education curriculum in Northern Ireland. The Report clearly demonstrates that even before the appointment of Martin McGuinness as Minister of Education the direction of policy for the education of children in Northern Ireland was in the hands of the barbarians.

Devolved government for Northern Ireland

Devolved government for Northern Ireland must be based on the intrinsic merits of unionism and not, as in the Belfast Agreement, on the appeasement of 'Irish republican' terrorism. The political content of unionism was set out in the Solemn Covenant of 1912 as 'the cherished position of equal citizenship in the United

Authentic Unionism

Kingdom'. A devolved system of government based on unionism must, of course, consolidate the Union as the only political context that can ensure the economic and social well-being of the citizens of Northern Ireland. The notion of citizenship is central to unionism. This distinguishes unionism from the ethnic allegiance to an imagined 'nation' that lies at the heart of Irish nationalism. This means that a devolved system of government for Northern Ireland must be based on the substantive content of the notion of citizenship.

The notion of citizenship derives its substantive content from the normative ideals of democracy and the rule of law. The normative political content of the requirements of the rule of law is that the operation of the criminal law must not be determined by political opportunism such as the appeasement of terrorism required by the Belfast Agreement. This means that the Belfast Agreement is entirely incompatible with the substantive understanding of citizenship that lies at the heart of unionism. Devolved government for Northern Ireland based on the intrinsic merits of unionism must have as its foundation an authentic commitment to the requirements of the integrity of the rule of law.

Unionism is based on an understanding of citizenship that gives a central recognition to the right to diversity of viewpoint or, in the traditional language of unionism, the right to civil and religious liberty. This is the basis of the unionist commitment to democracy as the political system that best guarantees the right to civil and religious liberty. But this understanding of democracy must not be confused with the intellectual and moral nihilism which demands that democracy must be open to an unrestricted accommodation of diverse viewpoints. For example, the view of Patrick Pease that 'blood-shedding is a cleansing and sanctifying thing' should simply not be tolerated in a democracy. 'Pluralism' that requires unrestricted tolerance is erosive of the public morality required to sustain democracy. The political influence of this type of 'pluralism' gives rise to a perverse political pragmatism unconstrained by the imperatives of the civic virtue that the operation and survival of democracy actually requires.

This unprincipled pragmatism is now rampant in the politics of the United Kingdom. That is why virtually the entire House of Commons applauded as democratic a system of devolved government for Northern Ireland that is a straightforward accommodation of the Sinn Fein/IRA ideology of terror. But unionists in Northern Ireland have not lost an authentic sense of propriety - of what is right and proper - in government and politics. Unionists must have the self-confidence to totally reject a system of devolved government in Northern Ireland that is an insult to common decency. Unionists need not regard this rejection as something negative but rather as a positive contribution to a restoration of the public morality and civic virtue required to sustain democracy in the United Kingdom.

Further, the recognition of the right to diversity of viewpoint must not be extended to incorporate the requirement that citizens give 'parity of esteem' to political commitments with which they disagree. The inability of nationalists to back their political demands with coherent and persuasive argument is the underlying reason for the nationalist demand that unionists must extend 'parity of esteem' to Irish nationalism. What is the substance of this demand by nationalists for 'parity of esteem' for Irish nationalism? The substance of this demand is the requirement that unionists must not merely respect the right of nationalists as citizens to hold their political viewpoint but that unionists must treat nationalism as intellectually and morally equivalent to unionism. This is simply an intellectually absurd demand which unionists must not feel under any obligation to meet.

Unionists must cultivate the self-confidence to resist the nationalist demand for 'parity of esteem'. This would be entirely compatible with unionist respect for the rights of nationalists as citizens. The nationalist demand for 'parity of esteem' for Irish nationalism has a political purpose. The purpose is to use this demand to divest Northern Ireland of its symbolic and substantive identity as an integral part of the United Kingdom. That is why the use of the education system to inculcate the nationalist understanding of 'parity of esteem' is a core requirement of *Towards a Culture of Tolerance: Education for Diversity* which states that:

> The Group felt that 'tolerance' is too feeble a term to express the values of inclusiveness, mutual support and appreciation among all of the elements of our society which should be placed at the heart of our community and embodied in the education system. The Group would suggest that our society, at its best, should not be satisfied to have its children 'put up with one another', but will wish for the development in them of an active and informed respect for and appreciation of, the variety and rich diversity of our cultures.

This is in fact a blueprint for the type of indoctrination that the authors of the Report considered was necessary to secure the long-term implementation of the Belfast Agreement. The proposal is the very antithesis of education. One of the central concerns of education is to develop in children and students the capacity for critical evaluation and discernment in the assessment of competing viewpoints. Contrary to the DENI Report democracy requires no more than a tolerance of competing viewpoints subject to the constraint of the need to cultivate the public morality and civic virtue required for the operation of democracy.

In fact, democracy is a system of government that does not merely accommodate but best thrives on the clash and competition of ideas. Democracy is the political accommodation of creativity, innovation and intellectual conflict and this understanding of democracy is entirely compatible with unionism. That is why unionists must refuse to accept a system of devolved government based on the moronic conformity required for the forced consensus without which the Executive established under the Belfast Agreement could not operate. Northern Ireland requires a system of devolved government appropriate to the pragmatic requirements of a population of 1.5 million. This would fundamentally involve keeping Northern Ireland within the United Kingdom. Unionists must not accept a system of devolved government based on the morally insulting pretence that terrorists are democrats in order to meet the ideological requirements of Irish nationalism.